Apple Watch Guide: Manual to Unleash Your Smartwatch!

By Shelby Johnson

Disclaimer:

This eBook is an unofficial guide for using the Apple Watch and is not meant to replace any official documentation that came with the device or any online instructions provided by Apple. The information in this guide is meant as recommendations and suggestions, but the author bears no responsibility for any issues arising from improper use of the Apple Watch. The owner of the device is responsible for taking all necessary precautions and measures with their device.

Apple Watch, iPhone, Apple iPhone and Apple are trademarks of Apple or its affiliates. All other trademarks are the property of their respective owners. The author and publishers of this book are not associated with any product or vendor mentioned in this book. Any Apple Watch screenshots or images are meant for educational purposes only.

Special Bonus with this Guide

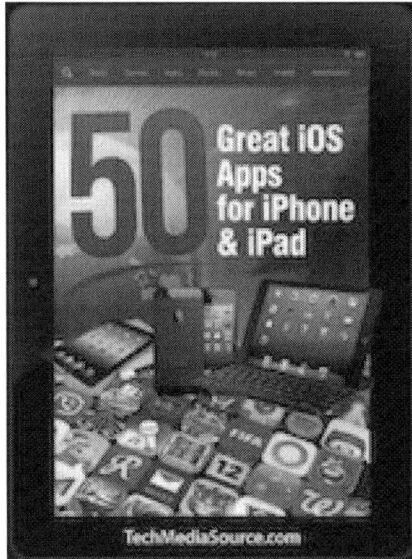

As a special thank you for purchasing this eBook, we are offering "50 Great iOS Apps eBook" for free **at TechMediaSource.com**!

Table of Contents

Introduction

Long gone are the days when a wristwatch simply tells us the time. With the introduction of a new mobile device, known as the smartwatch, technology companies are making sure the people and information we need on a daily basis are even more accessible than ever. The Apple Watch is now leading the way into the future as more users begin to embrace the concept of wearable technology.

The newest smartwatch by Apple was first released to the public in the spring of 2015 in a variety of formats including the affordable Apple Watch Sport, a mid-priced Apple Watch, and also the higher-end Apple Watch Edition. Prices range from $350 up to $10,000 for the highest end model. The watches were created for Apple iPhone owners to be able to integrate the smartwatch along with the apps and functions they use the most on their phone. There are even a variety of tasks that can be done when the Apple Watch is without the iPhone.

The biggest features on the Apple Watch include special notifications, the ability to control music or movies on compatible devices, the ability to track your daily or routine fitness goals, as well as functions for sending and receiving text messages, viewing emails, or even making and receiving phone calls. The watch tells time, provides important calendar dates, measures your heartbeat, and helps keep your physical fitness on track, while keeping you in touch with your most frequent contacts. There are also plenty of great third party apps on the market with Apple Watch integration.

The Apple Watch has a bit of a learning curve once you strap it onto your wrist. Inside this unofficial user guide, we'll provide you the instructions, tips, and tricks that you need to get even more from your Apple Watch in your daily life. We'll look at the basic set up, the customization, operation, and other aspects of this innovative smartwatch to help make this latest item even more user friendly in your daily life! We'll get started by familiarizing you with the product and it's overall set up.

Watch Pre-Setup

Before you begin set up of your Apple Watch, make sure you have several things ready to go. These include your Apple Watch and your compatible iPhone. Apple Watch works with iPhone 5, 5c, 5s, 6, or 6 Plus and iOS 8.2 mobile operating system. You'll also want to have your Apple ID username (or email address) and password handy.

Sign up for iTunes/App Store/iCloud

If you don't already have iTunes, App Store and iCloud account access, you need to sign up. These particular accounts and services will be an integral part of your experience between your Apple Watch and your iPhone.

To sign up for iTunes/App Store/iCloud, which you have to do to get the most from your device, you simply need an email address, your choice of a password, and your contact information to set the account up online. You will also need a valid credit card or PayPal account, and you will have to include that information in your account set up.

iTunes will not charge your account unless you make a purchase, but it does require a default payment method that is up to date at all times. This allows you to update apps, download music, movies, and iBooks – even if they are free. Your account will ask you to sign in by entering your password before any downloads can take place, and without a valid payment option – even if you are downloading free stuff – you will not be able to proceed with everything your account has to offer. While you won't be purchasing or downloading with your watch, you'll be using your iPhone with the Watch, so you'll want to have the options available.

What's in the Apple Watch Box

When you purchase your new, sleek and exciting Apple Watch, and carefully open the heavy-duty white box and inner packaging, you will find:

Apple Watch: The watch will be encased in a plastic packaging inside the box.

Extra wristband: You will have a second wristband piece also included inside the box.

Charging cable: The cable has a standard USB output on one end, which will fit directly into your computer or other device that has a USB input. The other end is much different than what normally accompanies Apple devices as this cable features a circular magnet that your Watch will sit on to recharge.

USB Wall Charger: The charger will plug directly into a standard AC power outlet, while the USB cable attaches to base of the adapter on one end and the watch rests on the magnet of the charging cable.

Paperwork: Included in the box is a bundle of paperwork including Apple stickers, warranty details, quick instruction papers, and a diagram of the Apple Watch.

That's all there is to it! Of course, you may decide you want extra accessories to go with your purchase. We'll cover those towards the end of this guide, as there are some great options out there to take your watch to another level.

Apple Watch Setup

After carefully removing all items from the packaging, make sure the watch can be securely fastened around your wrist. Consult the instruction guide that came with the watch. It shows exactly how to wrap the band around your wrist and secure it properly.

The Apple Watch may have some power when you first get it, but you should charge it more before you use it.

1. Plug in the USB charger to the included wall charger.
2. Plug the wall adaptor into an available socket.
3. Line up the back of your watch onto the circle's grooved side of the charging cable. The watch should indicate it is charging. Allow the watch to charge for a short while and then you're ready to start setup.

Pairing Apple Watch with iPhone

You'll need to pair your Apple Watch with a compatible iPhone. You must have the Apple Watch app already installed on your compatible iPhone in order to pair it with the watch. Also, ensure sure you have updated to the latest system update in your iPhone settings. Once you have the app installed, you'll need your Apple Watch and iPhone near each other to start pairing.

1. First, power your watch on with the long side button. You should see the Apple logo appear. The phone will take a few minutes to power up.
2. Tap on the preferred language, i.e. English, Spanish, etc.

3. Tap on the Apple Watch app on your iPhone to open it.
4. Tap Start Pairing on your Apple Watch.

You will have two options to pair the watch:

Pairing Option 1

Hold your watch up so it is aligned with the viewfinder in the center of your iPhone screen. This may take several moments before the iPhone app detects the watch so be patient. The watch will eventually give you a screen saying the watch has been paired.

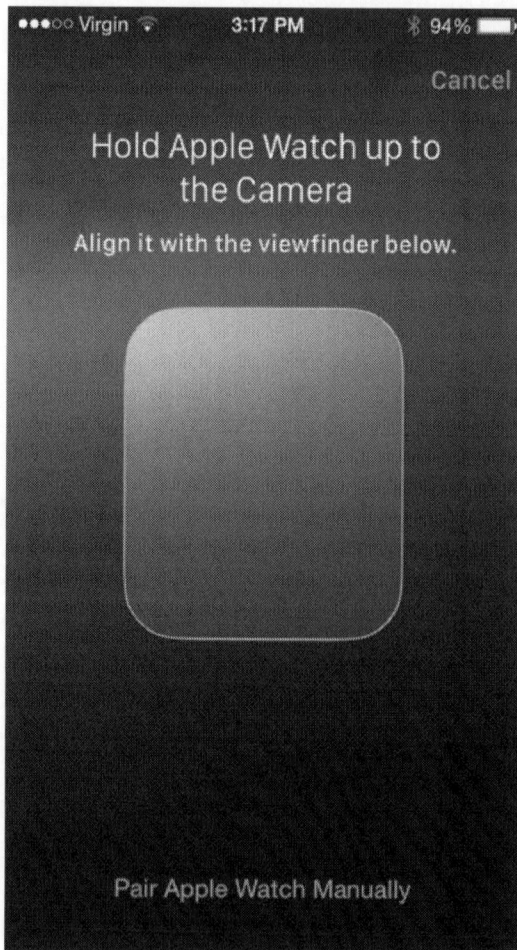

Pairing Option 2

1. A second way to pair the watch with your iPhone is to tap on Pair Apple Watch Manually. You'll see a screen with instructions to tap on the "i" icon on your Apple Watch to view its name.
2. Tap on the corresponding Apple Watch name that shows on your iPhone app screen.
3. Your iPhone app will prompt you to enter a 6-digit code that you should see on your watch. Enter this code to finish pairing the watch and iPhone.

Note: If you tap Back on the screens after you've paired your watch with your phone, you'll soon get a Pop-up warning message telling you that "Going back will unpair devices and reset Apple Watch to factory settings."

Setting Up Apple Watch

Now that the Apple Watch is paired with your iPhone it is time to go through the set up of the Watch to get your apps and information synchronized.

1. Once you have paired the watch and your iPhone, tap on Set up Apple Watch to resume set up.
2. Tap on Left or Right for the wrist you plan to wear your Apple Watch on.
3. Read Terms and Conditions, then tap on Agree to move forward. Tap Agree on the pop-up message box.
4. Enter your Apple ID email and password. Your login will be verified. You can also choose to Skip This Step by tapping on the words at the bottom of the screen.
5. Tap on Ok on the Location Services screen to move forward. Location services will help apps on the watch and/or your

phone to give better features based on your approximate location.

6. Tap on Ok on the Siri screen to enable Siri voice interaction on your Apple Watch.

7. Tap on Ok for Diagnostics, if you'd like to send reports to Apple about your diagnostic and usage date. You can always change this setting under Privacy.

8. Create a 4-digit Passcode to provide security for your watch when you take it off. You can also opt to create a longer passcode if you desire.

9. On your Apple Watch, choose Yes or No, as to whether you want the watch to unlock when you are wearing it and you've unlocked your iPhone.

10. Next you can choose to Install All available apps for your watch, or tap on Choose later. If you tap on Install All, you will get an "Apple Watch is Syncing" screen. Your watch will display the Apple logo and a progress meter around it, like a clock face. You'll receive an alert when the watch and your phone have finished this process.

Note: *Once you've finished syncing the Watch apps with your iPhone you may see messages on a compatible Apple MacBook or Apple computer alerting you that certain apps are now connected to Apple Watch. These may include Messages and iCloud.*

Customizing the Apple Watch Display

The Apple Watch has a variety of unique displays you can use for your watch face. They include Utility, Modular, Simple, Motion, Astronomy, Color, Solar, Chronograph, Mickey, and X-Large. To access the different displays and choose one, you press down on your Apple Watch's main display screen. You can then scroll side to side between the various display options. The following image shows the Modular watch face and its customization screen.

There is also a Customize button you can tap underneath any of the watch faces you'd like to use. Tap this to modify aspects of the layout such as the colors, sizes, and types of information presented on your watch display. For example, tapping Customize under the Mickey display lets you modify what information is displayed in the two small boxes on the top corners of the display and the long bar across the bottom of the display.

Some of the different information you can display on your main screen includes stock quotes, weather, world clock times for different locations, stopwatch, timer, alarms, or battery percentage. Simply tap on the box or shape on the display screen and then turn the dial on the side of the watch to change what information is displayed. When finished, you can press the side dial on your watch twice to return to the main screen.

Watch Buttons, Navigation & Notifications

Navigation on the Apple Watch is done with swipes of your finger on screen, or by using the Digital Crown (side dial) on the watch or the Long button on the side. You may prefer swiping the screen or using the dial and buttons to perform certain actions. In addition, it is important to know where to access notifications – by swiping from the top of your watch display.

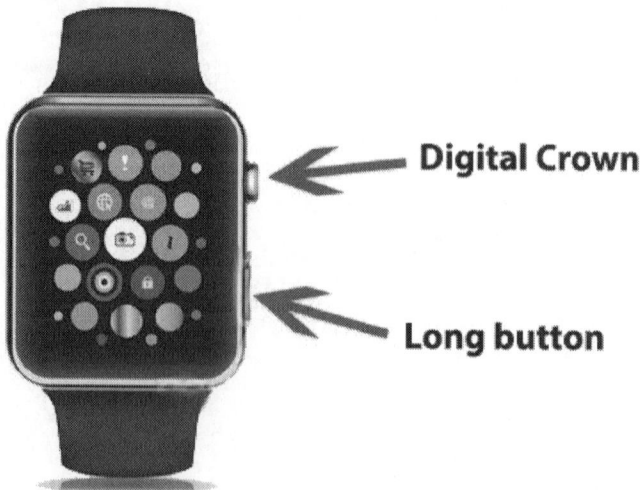

Digital Crown

Long button

Waking the Watch Display: Normally, to wake up your display from being asleep, you can press either side button. A finger tap on the watch screen can also wake the display. You can also set the display to wake when you raise your wrist, which will be described a bit later in this guide.

Once your watch is awake and you have entered your passcode (if you have one set), you can perform different actions by using taps, swipes, or hard presses of your finger on the watch screen.

Swipe Up from Bottom of Screen: You can swipe up from the bottom of the display to reveal Glances – quick looks at information from the apps you want to see. You can use your finger to swipe side to side between these Glances screens.

Swipe Down from Top of Screen: You can also see any of your latest notifications by swiping from the top of the watch screen down. These may include unread text messages, missed phone calls or other important information.

Finger swipes, taps and more: Swiping from left to right and vice versa on the watch display will move between various screens. Swiping up or down on various app screens allows you to scroll through options or items. Generally, you'll use a tap of your finger to make on screen selections. You can also use your finger to drag and drop in some instances.

Finger Hard Press: Another action you can use on many screens is a hard press with your finger. Often times this will allow you to edit, customize or perform other actions within the app or screen.

Side Button Uses: As mentioned there are two buttons on the side of your Apple Watch: a Digital Crown and a long flat button (as seen in the preceding image).

The Digital Crown (side dial): This dial can be used as a scroll type adjustor for certain things including volume or scrolling up and down between options or items on an app screen. It can also be pressed in to get to your apps group screen or other screens on the watch.

Double tap the Digital Crown from your main screen to bring up the last app you were using on your Watch. Double tap the Digital Crown again to return to the main screen.

Press and hold the Digital Crown when your watch display is awake to activate Siri.

Long Side Button: This button can be pressed or held in for a variety of actions. Press the long side button from your main watch face display screen and you'll bring up the contacts you are most connected with. These are generally the contacts you've been calling or sending messages to the most.

Double tap the long side button to bring up Apple Pay on your watch.

Press and hold in the long side button on your watch (when it is awake and unlocked) to bring up the following options: Power Off, Power Reserve, or Lock Device. You can then tap on any of these choices.

As you can see, the simple finger gestures and side buttons have many uses. This guide will go in more depth about which navigation actions or buttons do what in the coming sections.

Using the Apple Watch Apps

The Apple Watch includes a host of great apps that will be installed to work in conjunction with your iPhone. Bringing up your apps group on the watch is as simple as tap pressing the Digital Crown (side dial) once. You will see all of the installed app icons. You can move the group around using your finger on the display and tap on any app icon to open it. The Digital Crown can also be turned to adjust the size perspective of the group of apps. The following image shows the group apps screen on the watch.

Installing a new app is easy, because compatible apps automatically get added to your Watch after you install them on your iPhone.

Here is a look at how to use the various apps that may show up on your Apple Watch.

1. To access the apps screen on your phone, press the circular dial on the side of your phone in. Press the dial again to return to main time screen.
2. Tap on the app you want to use to open it.

Note: When on the apps group screen, turn the side dial to adjust the size perspective of the group of apps.

The apps you have installed should already be synchronized with the settings you are using for these apps on your iPhone. That means when you tap on an app on your watch, it will bring up the information that you have in the app from your iPhone. For example, the Stocks app will show any stock tickers and quotes that you set up on your iPhone, or the Weather app will show the current weather for your location, as previously set up on your iPhone.

To uninstall an app from your Apple Watch, simple press and hold down on the app icon (on the app groups screen of your watch – seen in preceding image). All of the apps will start to wiggle. You can tap the tiny "X" on any app icon to delete it from your Watch. Keep in mind the app will still remain on your phone, unless you also go in and delete/uninstall it on your iPhone.

Weather – Tap on the weather app (cloud w/sun icon) to bring up the current weather for your location. You can scroll side to side on your watch screen with your finger to see any other locations you may have set up on your iPhone weather app. Scroll down on the screen for any location to see the 10-day forecast for the region.

You can also change what information is displayed for your weather report on the display. Press down firmly on any location's screen and it will bring up three options: Condition, % Rain or Temperature.

Condition will show you what the weather is expected to be at each approaching hour over the next twelve hours (i.e. sunny, cloudy, rain, etc.).

% Rain will show you the percentage chance of rain each hour over the next twelve hours of the day.

Temperature will simply provide you the expected temperature outside for each hour over the next twelve hours of the day.

Note: If you want to change the locations you receive weather information for, you will need to adjust this on your iPhone or compatible Mac computer.

Calendar – The Calendar app on your Apple Watch is synchronized with Calendar on your other compatible devices including your iPhone, and possibly your iCloud. The calendar will show you anything occurring or scheduled on the current day and any upcoming items within the next few days. You can also view the calendar for the full month and then tap on any date to see what events or reminders might be there.

Camera – With the initial camera app on your watch, you can use the watch as a remote to activate your iPhone's camera. You can take a quick shot, or set a countdown timer to take a shot from your iPhone when ready. This can be helpful to take a timed selfie where you are trying to get the right pose, etc.

To take a quick photo, tap on the small white circle at the bottom center of the screen. You'll hear the camera shutter sound effect as the photo is taken. You'll see the photo on the lower left corner of your watch. Tap on the photo to view it larger on your watch and then tap close to close the photo. This photo will be stored on your iPhone.

To use the timer feature, tap on the small circle with "3s" in it on the lower right area of your watch screen. You'll see a view of the scene or image you're trying to take a picture of on your watch screen. The watch will show a visible 3 and then 2 and 1, along with a sound effect, indicating it is going to be taking the photo.

Note: Keep in mind that the photos you take using the Watch are stored on your iPhone. You will need to delete them from the iPhone, as there is no current way to delete them using your watch. Also, Apple Watch camera app currently is unable to record videos from the iPhone.

 **Maps –** The maps app will help you find your way around whether on foot or in a car. A cool aspect of this particular app is that if you are using turn-by-turn directions on foot, the Apple Watch will notify you when you need to make a turn by pulsating/buzzing your wrist gently.

In order to use the map to help you get to a location:

- Tap on the maps app icon to open the app. It will determine your current location on the map.
- Give a hard press on your display screen with your finger. That will bring up two choices: Search or Contact.

Tap Search to use your voice to dictate the place you're trying to get to, or you can scroll among any recent locations you've used that are listed on screen.

Tap Contacts to select a person or place from your contacts list. This is obviously best for contacts you have stored address information for.

- Once you've selected the person or place you want to find, tap on that person or place. (In the case of a "Search" you may first have to choose from a listing of different locations and their addresses)
- The app will bring up options for walking or driving with estimated times it will take for each method. Tap on either choice, and then tap on "Start" on your screen to begin using Maps to direct you to your location.
- Screens will come up one-by-one as you travel along the route directing you how to proceed. As you need to make turns, the Apple Watch will also provide a sensation to your wrist to notify you.

Note: You can also hard press on the screen during map directions at any time and bring up options to Stop (stop the Map directions help) or Contact, to call the personal/place you are trying to get to.

Music – The music app allows you to choose from the albums, artists, songs and playlists that are associated with your iPhone. For the most part, you can use this app to control playback of the music from your iPhone. You can also store certain playlists on your Watch so you can listen to those songs from your Watch (without needing your iPhone around). This is covered later in the Tips and Tricks sections of this guide.

To use the Music app, you can swipe and tap the screen with your finger to scroll between screens or make selections. You can view your available music by tapping on Artists, Albums, Songs, or Playlists. Tap on any of the available song choices to bring up the playback screen.

When playing a song, use the on screen back/forward buttons, as well as the pause/play button to control song playback. You can also use the Digital Crown (side dial) to scroll, or adjust the volume during song playback.

Email – The Apple Watch allows you to view your latest email messages (in association with your iPhone). You can scroll through the emails, tap on any of them, and read them. Also, when scrolling through your list of emails you can drag any email to the left side of your screen. It will bring up some helpful options.

You can tap on More for several helpful email options. These include Flag to flag the email as important, or Mark Unread, to keep the email fresh in your inbox.

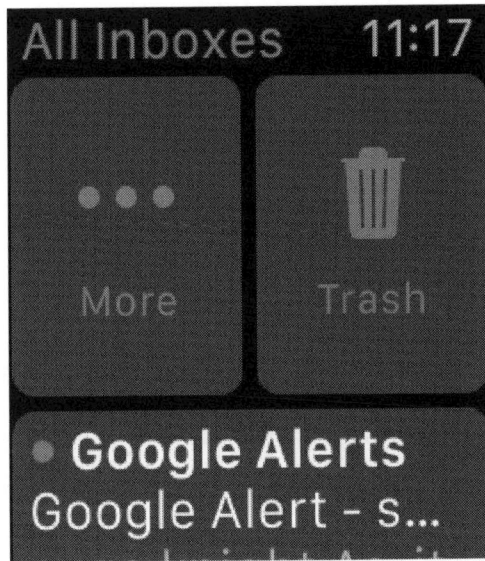

The other option you will see is a red trashcan. Simply tap on this and confirm you want to delete the email. This makes getting rid of all those spam or other unwanted emails cluttering your inbox a lot easier!

Phone – Use this app to make phone calls or check your latest voicemail messages. You can tap on your Favorites or Contacts to make calls to those individuals. Favorites are anyone you have marked as a favorite contact on your iPhone. Tap on Recents to bring up a scrollable list of anyone who you have contacted, or who has contacted you recently. You can tap on Voicemail to see a listing of all your voicemail messages. See the making a phone call section of this guide for more information.

Alarms – The Apple Watch can even serve as an alarm clock. Tap on the orange alarm clock icon and then press firmly on your screen. From there you can set up a new alarm with the time, how often to repeat and even name the alarm.

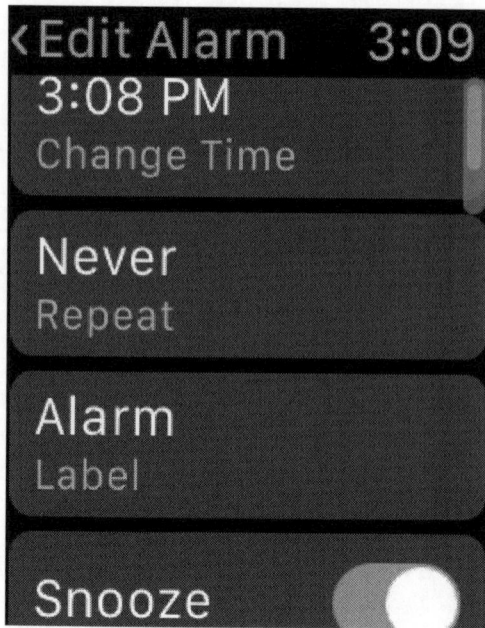

```
‹Edit Alarm    3:09
3:08 PM
Change Time

Never
Repeat

Alarm
Label

Snooze
```

You also have a "snooze" button slider at the touch of a finger. Keep in mind, you can set multiple alarms, and always go back into this app to edit or delete any alarms you no longer wish to use.

World Clock – Tap on the orange World Clock icon and it will show you the latest times from around the world, based on the geographic locations you may have previously set up on your iPhone or iCloud. Frequent travelers or those who make contact with people in different time zones will find this app to be quite useful.

Time – Tapping on the time app in your group of apps will simply return you to your main watch face display, showing the latest time and other information you have on the screen.

Stopwatch & Lap Timer – Perfect for runners who want to time laps is the stopwatch and lap timer app. You can tap on the Stopwatch app, and then tap on Start to begin timing your run. Hit the Lap button to start timing a separate lap. This is a very useful built-in feature for athletes.

Countdown Timer – Need to time something in the oven? This built-in app helps you set a countdown timer for any amount of minutes you prefer! Simply tap to set up a timer, then use the Digital Crown (side dial) to adjust to the number of minutes you want to count down from.

Workout Tracker – The Workout Tracker icon is the green circle with a person running inside. When you open this app, you can track your fitness in a variety of different workout settings as you're wearing your Apple Watch. For example, you can use this app to track a walk, a jog, or other type of physical activity you want to measure.

Move – This app will provide you with daily activity goals to engage your physical fitness. You'll need to supply some basic information such as your height, weight, sex and birthdate, as well as your activity level from low to high. Once you do, you'll receive specific goals for your day.

Four screens can be swiped for this app from left to right: Activity, Move, Exercise, and Stand.

- **Activity** shows you a circular chart that displays how close you are to achieving your three daily goals. Those goals are each reflected by the next three screens (Move, Exercise, and Stand).

- **Move** shows you how many calories you have burned for your daily goal.
- **Exercise** shows how many minutes out of 30 you have exercised for the day.
- **Stand** shows you how many hours of the day you have stood up for at least one minute.

You can swipe down or use the Digital Crown (side dial) to scroll down on any of these screens for more information.

Note: Keep in mind that the watch measures these things as you are wearing it, so it will not register activity when the watch is not on your wrist.

Messages – A great feature on the Apple Watch is the ability to send text or voice messages. You can activate this by tapping on the Messages app icon on your Apple Watch's apps screen.

Sending a New Message to a Contact:

1. Open the Message app. To send a new message, press firmly down on your Apple Watch screen.
2. Tap on the New Message icon that appears.
3. Tap on Add Contact and choose one of the two options at the bottom of the screen:

Option 1) You can tap on the Contacts icon at the bottom of the screen to view a list of all contacts you have stored in your iPhone/iCloud. You can scroll through these contacts by simply swiping down or up, or you can turn the dial on the side of your watch. Once you've found the contact, tap on them. The watch display will show you that contact along with their phone numbers and/or email addresses. Tap on the phone number or email of the person you want to message.

Option 2) You can tap the microphone icon to speak a name of your contact and have the Watch find the contact for you from your iPhone's contacts. For example, tap the microphone and say "John Smith," if that is the name of the contact you want to message. You should see the name appear on your screen to tap on as your recipient.

Selecting or Inputting your Message:

Once you added the contact you want to message, tap on the message field on your screen. You now have an option to send a quick message by scrolling through the pre-made messages you see on your screen. These include simple phrases such as "I'm on the way," or "Sorry I can't talk right now," "OK," and "Absolutely."

New Messa... 5:41	Cancel	Cancel
Add Contact	What's up?	RECENTS
Create Message	I'm on my way.	
	OK	
Cancel Send	😀 🎤	

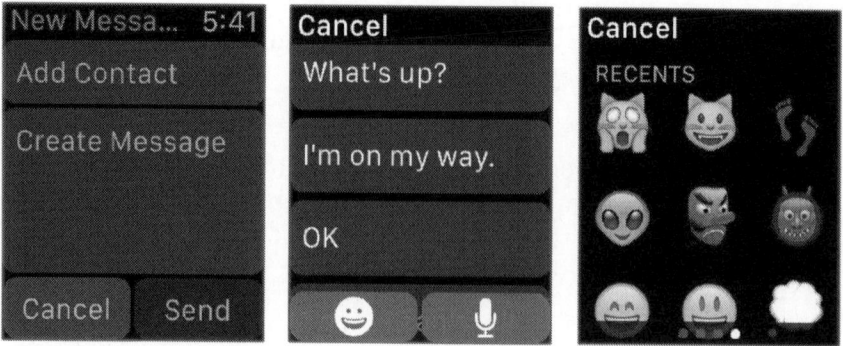

You can tap on one of these to send that as a quick message, or tap on one of the icons at the bottom of your screen as described here:

Option 1) Tap on the smiley face to select from different emojis or images to send quickly to your recipient. These may include a smiley face, heart and other quick pictures. It's important to note that the recipient may not be able to see the message if they don't have a compatible iPhone or Watch.

Option 2) Tap on the microphone to speak the message you want to send. The Watch will display your spoken text on the screen. Tap on "Done." You will be able to send the message as a text or recorded voice message. Tap on Send or you can tap Cancel if the message does not match what you want to send.

Other message options:

Once you've sent messages to several different contacts, you'll start to see the various messages listed on your Watch when you go to your Messages app. You can scroll through the messages using your finger on the display, or by turning the Apple Watch's Digital Crown (side dial). You can also bring up a few extras on any message conversation.

1. Tap on the message you want to review. For example, tap on your message with "John Smith."
2. Once you see the message conversation with that person, press firmly on the Watch screen.
3. This will bring up options such as "Reply," (to reply to the message) "Details" (for the Contact), or "Send location," to send the contact your current location from the Watch.

Remote – The remote app on your Apple Watch will allow you to use your watch as a remote control with your nearby Apple TV or an available iTunes library on your Mac computer or laptop. You'll need to make sure the Apple TV is switched on, or the iTunes Library is available for sharing to use this feature of your watch.

Settings App – This app icon (gears) on your Apple Watch provides you an extra bit of control over the features, apps and accessibility of your device. Tap on this to bring up the following:

Time: Tap on this option to set your clock face display time ahead. To do this:

Tap on the area of the screen where you see "+0 min" alongside the current time. You can adjust how many minutes ahead you want the clock face display to be by simply turning the side dial on your watch. Tap on the Set button at the bottom of the screen to set the clock display ahead by that many minutes.

To reset this option, you can always go back into this area of settings and tap on the area of the screen that shows how much time you set ahead (i.e. +5 min) and then use the side dial to move it to "0." Tap on Set to complete the reset.

Airplane Mode: Tap on this settings option to bring up the ON/OFF slider for Airplane Mode. Use your finger to move the slider to ON to put your Apple Watch into Airplane Mode, which shuts off wireless service. This is commonly used on airplanes where passengers are instructed to shut off their mobile devices.

You can always go back into the settings area and switch the slider to OFF to shut off Airplane Mode and resume use of your Watch.

Bluetooth: Tap on this settings option to begin searching for any nearby compatible Bluetooth devices. These may include select Bluetooth speakers, headsets or earbuds, and compatible health devices that you have. In order to find a device you may need to make sure that device has its Bluetooth setting on and is also "discoverable." Refer to any instructions included with the device for how to pair it with other devices.

Do Not Disturb: This option does just that – it makes sure you will not be disturbed through your Apple Watch, at least. Tap on the Do Not Disturb slider to turn it on. You will see a small colored moon on your Watch screen display now indicating it is on. You will not be disturbed by calls or alerts through the watch as long as this is switched on.

To turn the setting off, simply go back into Settings > Do Not Disturb and tap the slider to turn it off. The moon icon should disappear from your watch screen display.

General: This area of your Watch includes a variety of options to adjust or view. These include:

- **About** – Includes your Apple Watch name as well as other pertinent information such as the serial number, Model number, number of songs, number of apps, storage capacity, amount of storage used and more.
- **Orientation** – A settings area that allows you to change which wrist you will be wearing the watch on (left or right), as well as the ability to adjust the crown orientation. Adjusting this will flip the display upside down, or back right side up.
- **Activate on Wrist Raise** – A settings option that will give added convenience for waking your display. Switch the slider on this settings screen on and now whenever you raise your wrist up to view your watch, the display should automatically wake up. In this area, you can also choose what the screen will wake up with – either the main time screen, or the last app screen you were using before the display went to sleep.
- **Accessibility** - This settings area gives you access to adjusting Voice Over, Zoom, Reduce Motion and On/Off Labels.
- **Siri** – On this settings screen you can shift a slider to turn Siri voice assistance to On or Off. To use Siri on the Watch you simply say "Hey Siri" when the watch display is awake and speak your request. An example may be if you speak "Hey Siri, what's the weather?" and it brings up the latest temperature and conditions from your location.
- **Regulatory** – A simple screen giving the latest regulatory information for the United States and other participating countries.
- **Reset** – If you need to reset your watch to its original factory settings, this is the place to do it. Make sure you're absolutely sure before proceeding with this one though, as using this option wipes out all of your settings on the Watch (not your iPhone).

Brightness & Text Size: Tap into this settings area to adjust your display brightness using a slider, alter your text size on the display or use bold text.

Sounds & Haptics: Within this settings area, you can move a slider to lower or raise the volume for ringer and alert sounds. You can also mute them completely, although it will not silence alarms or timers if your Apple Watch is charging. Also in this area, adjust the intensity of haptics – the sensations you will feel on your wrist, such as gentle pulsating or buzzing, which help to alert you of new notifications.

Passcode: Within this settings area you can modify your passcode settings for the unlock security on your Apple Watch. Choose to disable it completely, or even set a slider to ON or OFF to unlock the watch with your iPhone.

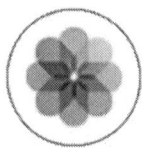

Photos: Use this app to view any photos you have synced from your iPhone. To sync the photos, you must go into the Apple Watch app on your iPhone. Tap on the Synced Album option to choose an album you want to store the photos from on your Apple Watch.

Also in the Apple Watch app on your iPhone in the Photos area, you can control how much storage space photos can take up on the Apple Watch. The initial setting on your watch is probably 15MB but you can increase this to your preferred amount. Your Apple Watch has an overall storage capacity of just over 6 gigabytes for all data (including synced music and photos).

Passbook: This app contains your participating loyalty/membership cards, movie tickets, sports or concert tickets, boarding passes, and any Apple Pay payment cards. You can activate the app from your Watch to present cards or ticket digitally at the participating merchants, restaurants and events. You can modify settings within your iPhone's Passbook app for this as needed.

Stocks: You can view the latest stock quote ticker information using this app. Stocks can be added or deleted from your list using the Stocks app on your iPhone or if you have it on your compatible Mac computer.

How to Add Apps to Apple Watch

Remember, adding apps to the Apple Watch is extremely simple. You only have to download the app to your iPhone and it is automatically added on your Watch. Third party apps need to be compatible with the Watch, but there are many apps already that have Apple Watch integration including the ones mentioned later in this guide.

If you finding that apps you install do not automatically get added to your Watch, go into the Apple Watch App on your iPhone. Tap on General and then tap on Automatic Downloads. Make sure the slider is switched ON for "Automatically Download Apps."

How to Delete Apps from the Watch

You may find that there are certain apps you don't want as part of your Apple Watch experience. Deleting these is simple as you press and hold down on the app icon (on the group apps screen for your Watch). All of the apps will begin to wiggle, similar to how they do on an iPhone or iPad when you do this. Tap on the small X on the specific app you want to delete to remove it from your Watch. The app will no longer be used with your Watch.

Note: Apps you delete on your Watch will remain on your iPhone. If you no longer want the app on your phone, you need to delete/uninstall them on the iPhone to completely remove them.

Using the Apple Watch App on Your iPhone

As previously noted, the iPhone has the Apple Watch app. This app contains key settings options and the ability to determine what apps you have active and how they interact with your watch. Tap on your iPhone's Apple Watch app icon to bring up a scrollable menu screen.

My Watch

📱　App Layout　　　　　　　　　>

✈️　Airplane Mode　　　　　　>

⌚　Apple Watch　　　　　　　>

📋　Notifications　　　　　　　>

📱　Glances　　　　　　　　　>

🌙　Do Not Disturb　　　　　>

⚙️　General　　　　　　　　　>

⌚　　　🧭　　　⭐　　　🔍
My Watch　Explore　Featured　Search

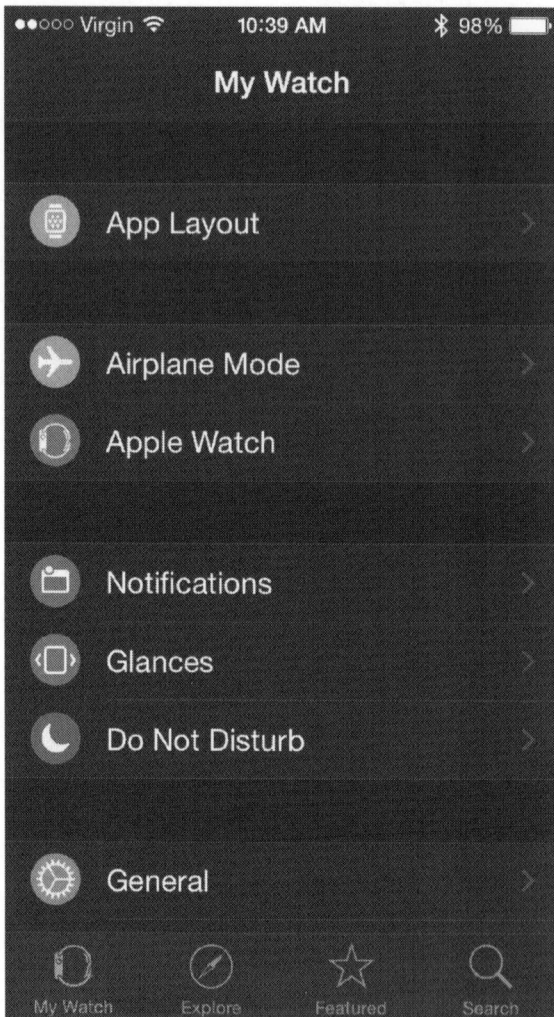

Tap on the Apple Watch app on your iPhone to access its settings and information. Here's what each of the options you see can do for your Watch and iPhone.

App Layout – You can adjust how your group of apps looks on your Apple Watch using this. Press and hold down on any icon with your finger, and then you can move it to where you prefer it in the apps group. The change will be made to the apps group on your Watch.

Airplane Mode – By tapping on this option, you can then adjust a slider for "Mirror iPhone." What this will do is mirror Airplane Mode between your Apple Watch and iPhone. For example, if you switch on Airplane Mode on your Watch, it will also get turned on for your iPhone, and vice versa.

Apple Watch – This area will tell you the name of your paired Apple Watch, as well as which watch it is. There's also a red option to "Unpair Apple Watch" here if you ever need it.

Notifications – This section allows you to customize which notifications are sent from compatible apps on your iPhone to those on your watch. You can also use sliders to turn off the notifications indicator that appears on your watch display (a small red dot) and turn Notification Privacy on or off. Notification Privacy allows you to tap on an alert from your app to get details, rather than the details automatically appearing for you.

Glances – When you swipe up from the bottom of your Apple Watch display, you activate Glances – quick views at the app information you want to see. This may include whatever song is playing, your battery level, stock info, weather, maps and more.

In the Glances area of the Apple Watch app on your iPhone, you'll find all of the active apps that are included. You'll see a red circle next to each one with a minus sign in it. Tap on that and you get the option to remove that particular app from the Glances screen of your watch.

In addition, you may see third party apps listed in the Glances area on your iPhone's Apple Watch app. Some may be listed under "Do Not Include." You can choose to include any app you want in your Glances on your watch by tapping on the green circle with a plus sign in it.

Do Not Disturb – You can adjust the slider to ON or OFF to mirror your iPhone for Do Not Disturb. If this setting is set to ON, your two devices will mirror one another when you turn on Do Not Disturb on either device.

General – This area contains a variety of settings and information for your Watch as described in the bullet list.

- **About** will show the watch name, version, model number, storage available on the watch, and more.
- **Software Update** is the area to check for and install any new OS updates for your watch. At the time of this first publication, OS 1.0 was the installed version
- **Automatic Downloads** allows you to adjust whether or not apps you install on your iPhone (that are compatible with the watch) will automatically install on the Apple Watch.
- **Watch Orientation** can be adjusted if you decide to use it on a different wrist, or want to adjust where the Digital Crown will be (on the right or left of the watch). The watch display will be flipped depending on which side you set the Digital Crown for.
- **Accessibility** provides a host of options that are generally helpful for those who may have vision and hearing impairments. For example, you can set up Voiceover to speak items on your screen, or turn on Zoom to allow you to zoom on your watch screen (by tapping two fingers). Other accessibility settings you can adjust include bold text, mono audio, gray scale and more.
- **Language & Region** allows you to set your watch's preferred system language, the region format and which calendar version you prefer. Many watches have these options set to English, United States and Gregorian, but these can be changed as needed.
- **Apple ID** simply displays the current Apple ID email or username you have associated with your Apple Watch.

- **Enable Handoff** is a slider that allows you to turn the handoff setting ON or OFF. When it is switched on, your iPhone will pick up with any apps right where you left off with the app on your Apple Watch. Switch the slider to OFF if you prefer to disable handoff.
- **Wrist Detection** features a slider to set the wrist detection ON or OFF. Wrist detection is a feature that allows your Watch display to wake up whenever you raise your wrist in the area. Having this setting on will make sure your watch stays locked if you are not wearing it.
- **Activate on Wrist Raise** allows you to adjust what happens when you raise your wrist. You can have the main watch face show or have the display show whatever previous activity you were using on the watch. For example, if you were using a certain app, the display will show that when you raise your wrist.
- **Usage** is an area that gives you information about the amount of storage your various apps and files on the watch are using. It will also show you how long it has been since you last charged the phone, as well as the watch's current standby and power reserve times.
- **Reset** is the option to use in the event you want to unpair your Watch from your iPhone and completely reset your Apple Watch. To do that, tap on Reset and then "Erase All Content and Settings." You can also choose to only reset your watch's home screen layout, or only reset Contacts and Calendar data that were synched from your iPhone to your Watch.

Brightness & Text Size – In this area of your iPhone's Apple Watch app, you can adjust overall brightness of the Apple Watch screen, increase or decrease the text size on the watch, and turn on Bold Text on the watch by switching a slider to ON.

Sounds & Haptics – You may decide you want to silence notification sounds, or turn the volume down for notifications that come from your Apple Watch. In this area of the iPhone app, you can move the volume meter towards the left to lower volume. You can switch the Mute slider to OFF to mute notification sounds completely.

You can also raise and lower Haptic Strength using the adjustable meter. Haptic Strength refers to the gentle buzz, tap or pulsating sensations you feel from the watch on your arm. You may receive these to alert you to text messages or other notifications. Slide to the far right for full strength, or slide far left for the lowest strength.

Cover to Mute can be switched on if you want to turn notification mute on by simply placing your palm over the watch display to cover it for 3 seconds (or more). Once you've enabled mute, you'll feel a tap from the watch to confirm it.

Prominent Haptic slider can be switched on if you want the Apple Watch to give you a sensation to pre-announce common alerts from your watch.

Passcode – Use this area of the app to turn the passcode on or off and change the passcode. There is also a helpful setting here in the event you misplace your watch or it gets stolen. You can switch a slider on next to "Erase Data." With this slider on, if someone tries to enter an incorrect passcode on your watch 10 times, Apple Watch will erase all data it has on it.

Health – Use this area of the app to adjust any information you've provided about your health for the Apple Watch. You can tap on Edit in the upper right corner of the screen and then adjust your birthdate, sex, height and weight, as needed.

Privacy – Here, you can adjust the settings for which apps are allowed certain information. For example, you may see the "Motion & Fitness" apps if you tap on that option. You can adjust sliders to ON or OFF for allowing Motion & Fitness to access your heart rate and body measurement.

Those are the standard settings inside your iPhone's Apple Watch App. After those you will see all of the other apps installed on your device, including any third party apps you may have installed that function with the Watch. You can tap on the various apps listed to modify their specific settings. Many of the apps may include sliders to turn iPhone mirroring with the app OFF or ON.

Using the Watch for Phone Calls

The Apple Watch allows you to make calls right over the watch. You'll simply find the contact you want to call and tap to make the call. The Watch will make the call using your iPhone, and then you listen to the call and respond over your watch.

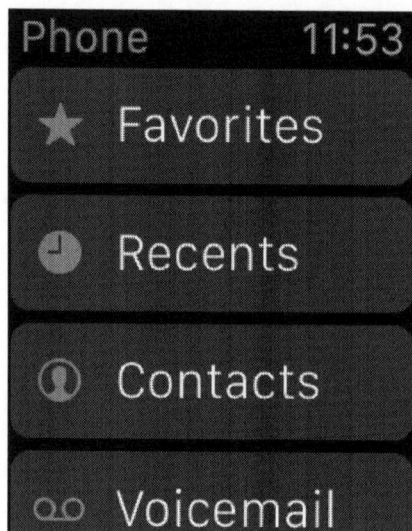

To make a call:

1. Tap on the Phone app icon.
2. Select Favorites, Recents or Contacts.
3. Tap on the favorite, recent call, or find and tap on the contact you want to call. The call will be made and you should hear the phone ringing through your Watch speaker.
4. Talk using the watch's built-in microphone and hear the caller via the built-in speaker.

You can hang-up by pressing the red phone icon at the bottom of the screen. You can also mute your voice at any time during a call using the mute icon at the bottom of the screen.

To answer a call:

1. Your watch screen will show you on the display who is calling you.
2. Tap on the phone icon at the bottom of the display to answer the call.
3. Talk using the watch's built-in microphone and hear the caller via the built-in speaker.
4. When finished you can tap the phone icon to hang up.

Note that there is also a mute button on-screen to mute your voice during a call.

How to Use Siri

Siri is a personal assistant that can be summoned to do "chores" for you, simply by asking her. Siri requires Internet access and can be awakened by simply holding down the "home" button – the main button of your device, at the bottom that contains a square – for a second. You will hear a two beeps, and Siri asking how she can help. You can ask her for the nearest Chinese restaurant location, or to call a friend who is listed in your contacts by simply saying, "Call Sarah Jones." She understands commands, so you do not have to talk like a robot to get her to respond accordingly.

What can I help you with?

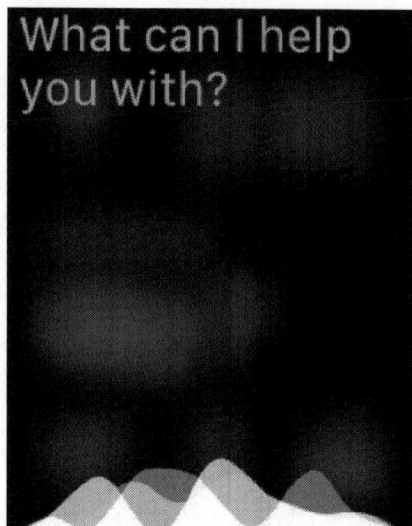

She can also compose a text message or read any messages in your inbox to you aloud. You can interact on social media just by telling her which platform to access, and typing the message you wish to display. She can also find a plumber, and dial their number if you command her to. She will set your alarm, set a timer, and add items to your calendar.

To use Siri on your Watch, the feature will need to be enabled in your Settings area. Go to Settings and General and tap on Siri, then adjust the slider button to ON if it isn't already. When your Apple Watch is awake, simply say "Hey Siri," to bring up the Siri screen. You can begin speaking your question such as "What is the stock quote for Apple?" or "What is the weather?" At times there will also be a microphone on screen which you can tap and speak your request. For example, you can say "Hey Siri, what's the weather?" and it will show you the latest weather for your location. If Siri doesn't understand what you are asking, a message will alert you on screen.

Turn off Siri on Apple Watch: To turn off Siri on your Apple Watch, go to Settings and General. Tap on Siri and then tap the slider button next to Hey Siri to turn it off.

Apple Watch Tips and Tricks

As you begin to play with your fun, new device, you will start figuring out shortcuts and options that you never knew existed. This is the nature of the beast with electronics. No matter how many manuals you read, or how many tutorials you sit through, practice really makes perfect with these devices, and sometimes trial and error does not hurt. For a few tried and true tips on operating your Apple Watch, check out the options below.

How Change the Watch Band

As mentioned in the suggested accessories section of this guide, you can easily swap or replace the band that comes with your watch. You'll want to make sure you swap it for a watch band of the same size, either 38mm or 42mm, but you can choose from the latest available bands for other watches besides the one you own. For example, you can purchase a stainless steel watchband to use with your Watch Sport model, as long as it is the same size band.

To remove the current band on your watch, simply turn your watch over. On the backside of your watch there are two small buttons near each part of the band. Press on these and slide the watchband out. This may take a bit of work to do, depending on which watch you have.

Take the new band you want to use with your Apple Watch and line up the two pieces with your watch to slide them into the watch. That is all there is to it. You have replaced your watchband with a different one.

How to Take a Screenshot

There may be some moments when you want to take a screenshot from your Apple Watch, perhaps to show someone your activity achievements on Move, or to show off a funny message you received.

To take a screenshot on your Apple Watch:

1. Make sure you are on the screen you want to capture.
2. Press and hold the long side button and at the same time, quickly tap on the Digital Crown (side dial).
3. You should see the screen flash and hear the camera shutter sound indicating you captured the screenshot.

You can find your screenshots stored in the Photos app on your Apple iPhone. You can now share that photo with others, edit it on the iPhone or delete it from your gallery.

Note: You may not be able to take a screenshot on all screens for your Apple Watch.

How to Measure Your Heartbeat

You can get a reading of your heartbeat at any time using the built in heart rate monitor. The Apple Watch has a special built-in sensor that rests on your wrist, when you have the watch attached around it. You will the Health app as part of the installed apps on your iPhone (this app was installed in a system update for iPhone 5 and 6 models).

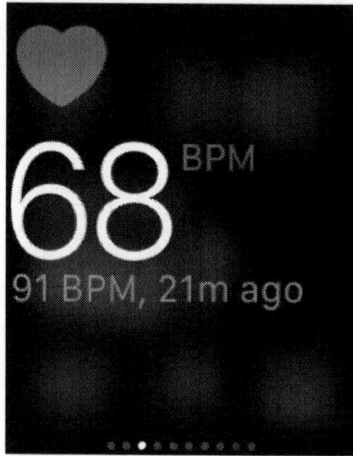

To get a heartbeat reading:

1. Swipe from the bottom of your display screen up (when watch is awake). This brings up your Glances screens.
2. Swipe right to left, or vice versa, until you are on the Heart screen.
3. Wait for several moments as the watch measures your heartbeat. The latest reading will be provided on the screen. The screen also displays the last reading that was taken and how long ago it was measured.

Note: If you cannot find the Heart screen, make sure that it is active in your iPhone's Apple Watch app settings.

How to Store & Play Music on Watch

The Apple Watch mostly works when you have your paired iPhone nearby, but there are a variety of things you can do when you are just using the Apple Watch alone. That includes listening to music, but it must be stored on the Watch. The Apple Watch features a total of 6.2 gigabytes of storage, and allows you to store songs on it until you have stored 2 gigabytes worth of songs.

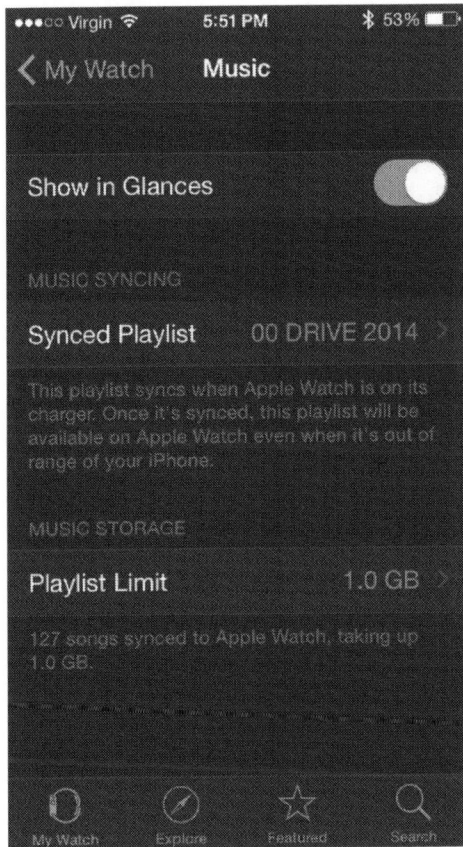

As of this guide's first publication, you can only add playlists of songs from your iPhone or iCloud to your Apple Watch.

1. Open the Apple Watch app on your iPhone.

2. Tap on Music.
3. Tap on Synced Playlist.
4. Select the playlist you want to synch on the Watch.
5. Wait for the playlist to synch to your Watch. Depending on how many songs are in the playlist, it may take some time to sync with your Watch. You'll see the percentage synced on your iPhone.

Once you have synched the playlist onto your Watch, you can now enjoy music with just your Apple Watch. You won't need your iPhone nearby to listen to the songs from the playlist from your watch.

1. While on the Music app on your Apple Watch, press firmly on the display until it brings up a few options.
2. Tap on the Source option.
3. Tap on Apple Watch. This will enable your Watch as the music playback source.
4. On your watch, go to the Song, Album, Artist or Playlist where you want to find a song to start playing. Tap on the song and it will begin to play from your watch. If you've got a Bluetooth headset, earbuds or speaker connected you should be able to hear the music through that particular item, if it has been paired via Bluetooth. Refer to any instructions with the device.

To get the most out of this feature, you should consider a good quality pair of Bluetooth earbuds, headphones, or a wireless Bluetooth speaker to play your music. There is more about those accessories later in this guide.

How to Use the Watch as an Apple TV Remote

You can use the Apple Watch to control your Apple TV right from the wrist. Once you have paired your items, your watch display becomes a touchpad to use for navigating on your Apple TV. Setting this up is quite easy, and obviously requires that you have an Apple TV to go with the Apple Watch.

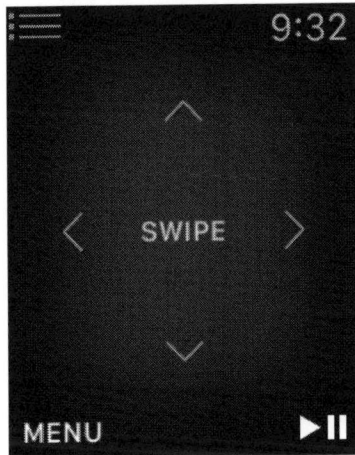

To set up your Apple Watch as a remote:

1. Make sure both the Apple Watch and Apple TV are powered on and that the Apple Watch is not in Airplane Mode.
2. Using your Apple TV's remote control, go to Settings, choose General, and then choose Remotes.
3. Choose your Apple Watch name listed on your Apple TV screen. (If it is not listed make sure to wake your Apple Watch display up and that you are in the Remote app).
4. The Apple TV will ask you to enter a special passcode. Using your Apple TV remote, enter the unique 4-digit code shown on your Apple Watch screen and choose DONE. The Apple TV will now show a symbol next to your Apple

Watch Name on screen to let you know the watch and Apple TV are paired.

5.   Go back into the Remotes app on your watch. You should now be able to tap on Apple TV to activate the remote. Your watch will give you a touchscreen remote to use for controlling your Apple TV.

To use the watch as a remote, you can now swipe your finger in different directions on your watch screen and that should control your Apple TV's on-screen navigation. You can tap on the watch face to make a selection on the Apple TV. You can also tap the "MENU" option on your watch screen to move back screens on the Apple TV, or tap on the Play/Pause icons to use those during playback of media on the Apple TV.

To unpair your Apple Watch and Apple TV, go back into your Apple TV Settings and choose General, then choose Remotes. Navigate down to where you see your paired Apple Watch name and select it to unpair it as a remote.

How to Use the Watch as an iTunes Remote

In similar fashion to using the Apple Watch as a remote for an Apple TV, you can also use it to control an iTunes Library from a compatible computer. It will allow you to control playback of music in the computer's iTunes Library and listen to that music via your watch wirelessly.

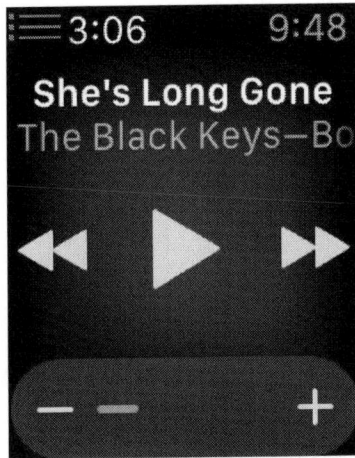

To set up the watch as an iTunes remote:

1. Open the Remotes app on your Apple Watch and tap on Add Device.
2. Open iTunes on your compatible computer and click on the Remote icon. You will probably see this in the upper left-hand corner for iTunes.
3. Enter the 4-digit code into iTunes. The code should be shown to you on your Apple Watch Remotes screen. The Watch will pair with your iTunes Library.

To use the remote, use the symbols on your Apple Watch screen in the Remotes app. Tap the play button to start playback, or the pause button to stop playback. Tap on the reverse or forwards buttons to navigate through the songs. Tap on the + or − symbols to adjust playback volume.

Note: Once you close down iTunes on your computer, it will disconnect the music library from being available with your Apple Watch's Remotes app. Once you re-open the iTunes on your computer, the Library should reconnect for use with your watch.

How to Modify Text Message Quick Responses

When you go to text someone, you'll have a list of various "quick responses" you can tap on to send as your message. These include simple words and phrases such as "Thank you," "Can't talk right now," "Absolutely" and "OK." You can change these quick responses by adding your own through your Watch app on your iPhone.

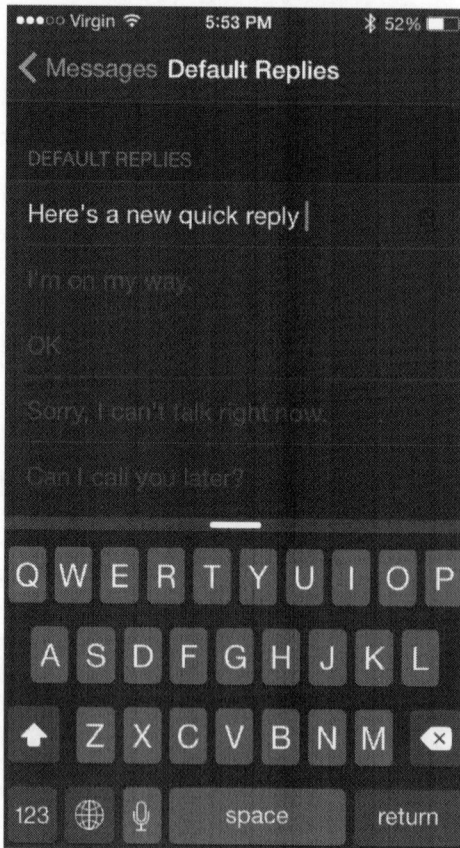

1. Open the Apple Watch app on your iPhone.
2. Scroll down to Messages and tap on it.

3. Tap on Default replies.
4. Tap on any of the messages you see and then use the iPhone's on-screen keyboard to input a message you want to use instead.

After you do this, any quick response messages you have changed will be available when you go into the Messages app on your Apple Watch.

How to Set up and Use Apple Pay

If you have an iPhone 6 with Apple Pay, you can also use this feature with your Apple Watch. The Apple Pay app should already be installed on your iPhone. Make sure to add your payment card (or cards) that you want to use on the app. You can use the feature at any merchant or vendor that offers Apple Pay.

To use Apple Pay from your Apple Watch, simply double tap the long side button on your Watch twice and then hold your watch face up towards the contactless reader.

You will feel a tap sensation and a beep from the Apple Watch to let you know your payment information was successfully sent.

For more information, see **apple.com/apple-pay** at the official Apple Website.

How to Unlock Your Hotel Room Door

Select hotels around the globe feature a special technology that allows you to use your Apple Watch as a key to unlock your hotel room door. As of this publication, the Aloft, Element, and W hotels use this technology, but others are likely to embrace it in the future.

To use this technology, install the SPG: Starwood Hotels & Resorts app on your iPhone. Make sure the app has also automatically installed for your Apple Watch.

1. Register through the app for SPG Keyless Registration.
2. Once you have an upcoming reservation at a participating hotel, you'll receive a push notification. You can choose to go keyless during your stay by using the Watch and the app.
3. Once your room is ready, you'll get a push notification with your room number and an option to unlock your door.
4. During your hotel stay, make sure your Watch is paired with your iPhone and Bluetooth is on for both devices.
5. When you need to unlock your hotel room door, you can tap on the "tap to unlock" button to use the mobile key from your Apple Watch's app. Make sure the watch is near to the door lock for this to work.

Note: Once you officially check out of the hotel, your mobile key will disappear.

How to Improve Battery Power

The Apple Watch battery power is supposed to last for 18 hours, but with a lot of use throughout the day, the battery can be depleted much more quickly than that. Aside from disabling the heart rate monitor or a bunch of your app notifications, there are some other things to try. The following sections have some good tips and tricks to help improve battery power while using the Apple Watch.

Activate Power Reserve

The power reserve is a helpful feature on your Apple Watch that lets you use the device in its simplest format – as a watch. When you activate this setting, tapping the side buttons to wake the watch will merely display the digital time on screen and nothing else. You will not be able to access any apps or other features in this mode, but it will conserve battery power.

To activate the power reserve feature:

1. Press and hold the long side button on your watch until you get a menu of three options.
2. Use your finger to slide the slider for Power Reserve to the right side.
3. The watch display will go to sleep. Now, whenever you wake the watch, the screen will only display the digital time.

You can also activate this mode from the Glances screen that shows your current percentage of battery power (if you have that particular screen active for Glances).

To exit from this mode, you will need to shut down and restart, or perform a reboot. Press and hold both the Digital Crown and the long side button at once for approximately 10 seconds. After a minute or so, the Apple Watch will reboot for normal use.

Use a Different Watch Face

There are a variety of watch faces you can choose for your display to show you the time and other information on screen. However, certain ones, such as the Mickey Mouse watch face, will eat up the battery quicker than others. The modular face is among the best for conserving battery power. To select a different watch face you simply hard press with your finger on your current watch face screen. The available watch faces will show up, and you can choose one and customize it.

Adjust Watch Screen Brightness

Consider lowering the brightness setting for your Watch display. You can do this inside the iPhone's Watch app. Tap on the Brightness & Text Size option, and then move the slider bar to the halfway setting or all the way to the left to lower brightness. On the watch, press the side dial (Digital Crown), tap on the Settings icon in your apps group, and then select Brightness and Text Size.

Reduce Motion and Transparency

You may want to reduce the motion and transparency settings on your Apple Watch, as the various animations that appear on the watch tend to drain battery faster. You can do this by going to your iPhone's Watch app and tapping on General. Tap on Accessibility and to reduce both the motion and the transparency to help preserve battery power.

Use the Grayscale Display

This will make your watch display in grayscale rather than the usual vivid colors. While the colorful display is nice, it is part of what affects the battery. To adjust the setting, go to the Apple Watch app via your iPhone and tap on General. Tap on Accessibility. Move the Grayscale slider from off to on.

How to Use Apple Watch for Home Automation

The Apple Watch is a smartwatch that will likely develop in the future as a convenient wireless tool. Part of that plan appears to be the ability to use the watch for various home automation tasks using on screen taps or Siri voice assistance. It was demonstrated during the initial reveal of the product that the watch could be used as a garage door opener, and as previously mentioned, the Apple Watch can be used for digital room entry at select hotels.

Currently, you can use home automation products that feature HomeKit compatibility. HomeKit is a special home interface system that works with Siri and your Apple Watch. There are already apps from Honeywell, BMW and Lutron that feature HomeKit that are compatible with the Apple Watch.

Some of the home devices that may be compatible with the Apple Watch in the future include power outlet controls, garage door openers, digital thermostats, light bulbs, keyless home entry and more. Stay tuned as these innovative new third party accessories become more available in the future.

Troubleshooting Apple Watch

Occasionally, you will experience some issues with your Apple Watch. The following sections have some troubleshooting tips and solutions for your Apple Watch.

Watch is not Working with iPhone

If you find that your Apple Watch isn't working with your iPhone, there could be a variety of issues. Here are the suggestions and ideas to consider:

- Make sure you have a compatible iPhone 5, 5s, 5c, 6, or 6 Plus.
- Make sure your Apple Watch and iPhone are both powered on.
- Make sure the Apple Watch is paired with the iPhone via Bluetooth.
- Check to make sure Airplane Mode is off for both the Apple Watch and the iPhone .
- Make sure the iPhone is within a reasonable proximity to the Apple Watch. Keep in mind that certain tasks require the iPhone within a reasonable distance. For example, you can have your iPhone in another room of your house as you are roaming around, but you cannot have the iPhone at a friend's house down the street and your Watch on your wrist inside your home.
- If it is a specific app that is not working, you will probably want to check into the app settings or notifications settings on your Apple Watch, or on your iPhone's Watch app.

Watch is not Charging

If you find your Apple Watch is not charging, don't panic. It could be one of the following that you need to check:

- Make sure the backside of your Apple Watch is properly seated on the charging magnet.
- Make sure that your USB cable is plugged into a working USB power source or outlet.

If you're finding that neither of these simple fixes address the issue, it may be time to consult with the Apple website, your local Apple Store or with the merchant you purchased the device from.

Specific App Issues

You may run into specific app issues or bugs while using the Apple Watch. Remember that only select apps are compatible with Apple Watch. For those apps that seem to be causing you issues, here are some considerations:

- See if there are any new updates for the app on your iPhone.
- Consider uninstalling the app from your iPhone and re-installing it from the iTunes App Store.
- Consider deleting the app from your Watch. You can do this by pressing your finger and holding down on the app icon on your Watch display. Wait for all of the apps in the group to wiggle on screen and tap the small "x" on the app to delete it.

Power off your Apple Watch

You may find that you need to power off your Watch completely if you want to save your remaining battery power, or perhaps to simply restart your watch to troubleshoot an issue.

To power off the Apple Watch:

- Press and hold the long side button on your Apple Watch.
- On the pop-up screen, move the slider for POWER OFF to the right side of your screen. The Apple Watch will shut down.

To turn your Apple Watch back on, you can press and hold the long side button. The Apple logo will display for several moments as the watch powers back on.

Rebooting your Apple Watch

A reboot is a simple troubleshoot you can try to fix issues. It can help you recover from errors by simply re-initializing the watch and its OS. A reboot will not wipe out your data.

To reboot the Apple Watch:

- Press and hold the Digital Crown and Long Side buttons at the same time.
- Wait about 10 seconds and then release both buttons. The watch should reboot, but may take a bit of time, so be patient.

Re-setting your Apple Watch

If you are having tremendous trouble with your Apple Watch, or are planning on selling the watch or transferring its ownership to another, you are going to want to restore the device to its original manufacturer settings. This will ensure that all of your personal information, music, contacts, and apps are deleted for good, so you can rest easy at night knowing that the person who bought it on eBay is not enjoying their daily latte using your virtual wallet.

Keep in mind that if you are doing this to fix a problem, you are wiping out the settings and data from the watch. You will not be erasing items on your iPhone by doing this.

When you are ready to reset the Apple Watch, follow these instructions:

1. Press and hold the long side button on your Apple Watch.
2. Slide the slider bar for "Reset" to the right side of your display.
3. Enter your passcode, if necessary, and confirm the reset by tapping on any confirmations, messages, or warnings

This process will restore the watch to its factory settings, so you are now free to get rid of it or to reload your data accordingly. It may also take a while to accomplish, rendering the watch useless while it proceeds with the complete reset. Once it has finished, the device will reboot and revert to the familiar factory setting screens that you completed when you first received it. At this juncture you have a couple of options:

- Leave it as is for the next person (buyer or gift recipient) to set up on his or her own.
- Re-pair with an iPhone and setup the device as a brand new setup for yourself.

15 Great Apple Watch Apps

On the surface, it seems the Apple Watch has just a select group of apps available, but don't be fooled. There are plenty of third party apps out there already, and more on the way. Here is a look at 10 different apps you may want to install for your Apple Watch right away. Remember, to install the app on your Watch, simply install it on your iPhone first and it will be added to your watch's apps group.

1. **TheConverted** – Check on common measurements and conversions on your watch.
2. **TheScore** – Sports Scores, schedules and stats for all the sporting events you care about.
3. **Yelp** – Scan local restaurant or business reviews and ratings, all from the tap of your watch!
4. **TripAdvisor** – The popular website's app helps you with restaurant or other suggestions for the location you are visiting.

5. **Elevate** – Use quick puzzles to test your wits right from your wrist.
6. **Pandora** – A helpful remote control app for using the Pandora music service on your iPhone.
7. **Twitter** – Check out recent tweets, favorite a tweet, retweet, and even send a tweet of your own using your voice to dictate on your Apple Watch.
8. **TV Guide**- Check the latest trend listings for what is on television to see what everyone is watching.
9. **Clear** – A $4.99 app that serves as a great To Do list. You can check off completed items on your watch screen and even add new To Dos using your voice. It also provides reminders as needed.
10. **Evernote** – A great synchronization with your Evernote app, this allows you to check over your latest notes and even record new ones using your voice.
11. **NYTimes** – Check out quick headlines or story summaries. This app will require a subscription to use. An alternative to this app is the USA Today app.
12. **Shazam** – The popular app that helps you figure out what song you are currently listening to also works for the Apple Watch (with your phone's microphone nearby). The neat bonuses are that once the song is determined you have options to view the song lyrics, or tap on Buy to buy the song from iTunes for your Apple iPhone.
13. **Starbucks** – Use this app to show a QR code that lets you pay for your Starbucks purchase. You can also view your latest earned rewards right on your wrist.
14. **Deliveries** – A $4.99 app that will allow you to track your latest package shipments that you are expecting from delivery. You can check on your wrist on a daily basis exactly what deliveries are expected to arrive.
15. **Yahoo! Weather** – Want to upgrade from the standard Weather app on your Watch? Look no further than this

Yahoo! Weather app that brings you even more detail and visuals about the latest weather.

Apple Watch Accessories to Consider

Your enjoyment of the Apple Watch should not be limited to just what is in the box. There are some great additional accessories on the market for use with the smartwatch, and more are being developed or unveiled as you read this. You can maximize the use and convenience of your watch with these upgrades for entertainment and power.

Apple Watch Bands

Want to change up the look of your Apple Watch? You can purchase different watch wristband straps to swap in and out with your Apple Watch. You'll want to get bands that are for the same size watch as the one you have, either 38mm or 42mm. However, you can select from available bands at the Apple Store including the stainless steel, buckle or other varieties, even if you have the Watch Sport that came with plastic bands.

See the latest available Apple Watch bands at http://store.apple.com/us/watch/bands

Wireless Bluetooth Speaker or Earbuds

Bluetooth, or wireless, speakers allow you to listen to music without all the mess of cables, so you can play music as a party or at home, without plugging into your iPhone. This is a great accessory to listen to the music from your iPhone while controlling it via your Watch.

Bose, Beats by Dr. Dre, and even the lesser-known Sono brand, all have wireless speakers, headphones and earbuds that you allow you to access them with your Apple Watch. Some great earbuds for runners or athletes include the Jaybird BlueBuds X Sport, 66 Audio BTS+, Monster iSport and the iKross Bluetooth A2DP Sport Sweat-proof models.

As always, make sure whether or not a particular earbud works with your device before making a purchase. Follow any included instructions with the item to hook it up to your Bluetooth.

Apple TV

The Apple TV is the revolutionary set top streaming media player that allows for enjoyment of movies, music, videos, podcasts, photos, and more on your television. Simply hook the Apple TV up to an available HDMI input on your hi-definition television and enjoy all sorts of great programming from free or subscriber-based services. These might include Netflix, Hulu Plus, YouTube, and even the iTunes Store's selection of movies you can rent or purchase. The Apple Watch works great as a remote control for the Apple TV as you can control it right from your wrist with ease. Consider this accessory to further automate your home entertainment system.

Portable Power Bank

A portable power bank will give you extended battery life for your Apple Watch, iPhone, and other USB compatible devices when you are on the road, whether it be a long trip by car, plane, train, or a cruise on the seas. One good power bank is the series of chargers by Anker Astro, as these devices include two power inputs on the front of the display, making it ideal to charge your Apple Watch and another device at the same time. Use it on that next long road trip to keep your device alive and extend the time you can use the device. These generally sell for under $50 depending on the capacity you buy, but keep in mind they'll weigh a bit and add to your accessories for packing.

Apple Watch Dock Stand

You can display your technology with a beautiful Apple Watch stand. Many companies are releasing different stands, some of which will help proudly show off your device while also charging it. However, you can really add to the look of a room's décor by adding any of the available watch dock stands!

Where to Get More Help for Apple Watch

If Apple has made one thing clear, it is that they like to be the troubleshooting resource for all of their products. Because of this shared mentality within the technological giant, the Apple website is a great source of information for product Q&A, troubleshooting guides and support.

Within their website they have online Apple Forums and Online Communities directly on their website, where you can submit a question and receive answers from Apple device users around the world. This is a helpful tool because there are a lot of different experiences that can be shared in one place, and the results are explained by a real person, rather than someone speaking tech talk and confusing you even further.

If the online communities with Apple.com are not providing you with the answers you need, simply locate the "Support" tab at the top of their website, choose the Apple Watch product when prompted, and search through any of the following resources for help:

- Videos.
- Manuals.
- Tech Specs.
- Online Support.
- Telephone Support.

When you need help now, and respond better to in the flesh support, you can visit a genius bar at your local Apple store. Genius bars are in-store help from real employees who know Apple products inside and out. They can offer advice, quick fixes and even suggestions for fixing your device whether it is under warranty or not.

To set up an appointment online, logon to their concierge service at the following URL: **http://concierge.apple.com/reservation/us/en/techsupport/**

Select your state, and the store you would like to make the appointment in from the drop down menus. Next, pick your device – in this case the Apple Watch. It may ask you to reboot your device, to see if that resolves your issue. It will also give you the opportunity to be re-routed to their online resources, or you can simply click "Continue with reservation" to get to the timeslots available.

It is HIGHLY recommended that you make an appointment at the Genius Bar, and do not simply show up at the Apple Store instead. Everyone (well, most) respects the system, and the Genius's time and knows that plowing through the line with your device will get you summarily rejected by the Genius you approach, and the scores of individuals politely (well, most) awaiting their turn. If you cannot make an appointment online, call the store nearest you to set one up over the phone. You will be glad you did.

Outside of the actual Apple sanctioned resources, there are thousands more online that can help you get through troubleshooting techniques that Apple may or may not approve of. Some of them are the same as what the folks at Apple will tell you, but maybe delivered in an easier to understand explanation.

Use your favorite search engine and ask the Apple Watch-related question that is plaguing you. You will receive answers from everywhere, including Apple, about.com, Amazon reviews, forums, online communities, and possibly retailers who are simply looking to sell you accessories.

The good news is, no matter what problem you are having, there is probably another Apple user who has experienced it too, and shared it with the world. This is what technology brings to the table: A worldwide forum of Apple users who can solve each other's problems online!

In all seriousness, look for help from a qualified and friendly Apple employee first. They are really great at walking you through steps over the phone or in an online chat. If all else fails, lean on the Mac world to give you a few pointers here and there. You never know, you may just learn something new about your device that you would not have known otherwise, and that is what it is all about!

Conclusion

The Apple Watch is an exciting smartwatch that includes plenty of great functions and features. Apple tends to offer great specs and features on its devices, which when understood, these features can really aid in comfort, day-to-day productivity, time management, and important situations. The wristwatch has come a long way since the days of simple wearable timepieces. Now, with a device that has so much power on your wrist, your life can be easier if you learn how to properly use your Apple Watch and take advantage of its capabilities.

The smartwatch can seem daunting and confusing at first, but over time you will become more comfortable with the gestures, actions, and functions that, excuse the pun, make it tick. Consult this guide as needed to get practice with using certain aspects of your watch, and you will soon be operating it like a tech pro.

Also, expect Apple to release important system updates for the Apple Watch in the future to address any bugs or add exciting new features. Also, there will be new accessories developed, as well as more third party app developers bringing new ways of interaction between your iPhone and your Watch. Each new app or update that becomes available for the Watch will help to give the watch more improved levels of convenience, ease of use, and of course, fun!

More Books by Shelby Johnson

iPhone 6 User's Manual: Tips & Tricks to Unleash the Power of Your Smartphone! (includes iOS 8)

iPhone 5 (5C & 5S) User's Manual: Tips and Tricks to Unleash the Power of Your Smartphone!

Apple TV User's Guide: Streaming Media Manual with Tips & Tricks

Yosemite OS X Manual: Your Tips & Tricks Guide Book

iPad Mini User's Guide: Simple Tips and Tricks to Unleash the Power of your Tablet!

Kindle Fire HDX & HD User's Guide Book: Unleash the Power of Your Tablet!

Kindle Paperwhite User's Manual: Guide to Enjoying your E-reader!

How to Get Rid of Cable TV & Save Money: Watch Digital TV & Live Stream Online Media

Chromebook User Manual: Guide for Chrome OS Apps, Tips & Tricks!

Chromecast Dongle User Manual: Guide to Stream to Your TV (w/Extra Tips & Tricks!)

Google Nexus 7 User's Manual: Tablet Guide Book with Tips & Tricks!

Samsung Galaxy S5 User Manual: Tips & Tricks Guide for Your Phone!

Samsung Galaxy Tab 4 User Manual: Tips & Tricks Guide for Your Tablet!

Amazon Fire TV User Manual: Guide to Unleash Your Streaming Media Device

Roku User Manual Guide: Private Channels List, Tips & Tricks

Facebook for Beginners: Navigating the Social Network

Printed in Great Britain
by Amazon.co.uk, Ltd.,
Marston Gate.